EXILED FROM STARS

EXILED FROM STARS

POEMS

JOSEPH M. GANT

REBEL SATORI PRESS
NEW ORLEANS

Published in the United States of America by
Rebel Satori Press
www.rebelsatoripress.com

Paperback ISBN: 978-1-60864-237-3
ebook ISBN: 978-1-60864-238-0

Contents

Kuddle

some of us
love teddy bears
full of glass
and tetanus,
hepatitis in the eyes
          tertiary needles.
pulling knives from memory
frost of blood
we plunge into the snow.

Commodities

I only write poems when I'm feeling unwell

this is a warning
this is the rule of the game we are playing

      I'm pouring over
            the pages of wine

and verses I tend to be selling today
a book for a dime
a nickel for your shame
a tedious pulling of teeth and of sinew
today I was bitten
by the dog that I love
I feed her
until she explodes on herself
I feed her until I can no longer pull
the day's less arrogant march—
a step to the heel,
a boot to the chin
I only write poems when I'm feeling unwell
and this was a warning that you failed to heed

Snap The Finger

unconditional and misguided
arms crossed
full of all the indignation
and defiance
heaven ever dared for us to carry
brown fingertips
my blistered thumb
and ash beneath my nails
extinguishing the mirror's shine
the novel ended there
where you passed the butt
of the gun and said
go first and I will swallow
and dreams of our forever
spin around inside the barrel

For Anne

we're here on Unit A again
where doors have fallen
walkways
I push my rusted walker to the courtyard
for generic smoke break
cancer that taste like tears
and broken legs

I tried to flee
on my donkey again
and here she is
the one-time queen
she pulls hard twice
exhales and smiles
another mistake
I look away
 13th stepping in the detox ward
never paid good dividends

I crack the spine
on a vinyl mattress,
throw my busted hip in bed
and try to read again

I used to bring Colossus
when I'd check in here
on Unit A
but Live or Die

I've graduated
lights out now
medications
never time to read.

Beta

pushing zeroes
and ones
through the veins
of god
like fentanyl dreams
and the dope show
we break /
reduced as sum
compiling cold pharmacopeia

Rehab

I cook
breakfast
with a guy
who did
five years
for stabbing
a friend
in a drug deal
he cuts cheese
for the eggs
with a stainless
blade
I mix
the batter
and sometimes life
is just pancakes

Surf

my eyes
have not adjusted
to the light we never were
waves that break
the bones of us
recede from tissues torn
I walk the day
and wonder while
the sun displays an poltergeist
bottles full of memories
buckets made of sand
pregnant with a dawn's becoming
nothing west of where we laid

Race

I don't walk
I fall forward
in log gray snails
Occam's razors cut the spine
and flays the rib cage like phantoms
this shirt is blue again
as it was last week
flannel of the tourniquet holds
meat and bone and tears together
I race towards the starting
line
to shelter or to storm
feet beneath two twigs that tremble
running where the track grows null

Death of a Geshe

eight years a boat
adrift in a long
dark sea
voices gone
faces gone
cannibalizing corpses
in the coldest
stretch of time
I meditate
and pray on darkness
death and a solitary king
fire like mountains
cradle the sky
where he left a body
illusory and silent
no teaching
no more
no guide to whatever
enlightenment might call
stamped with eternity-- postcard soul

She Stands Lightly

she stands lightly
by the glass
of the
door
green smiles from across the garden
and I watch
a groundhog
play tag
with blackbirds

the remainder follow suit

the afternoon rain
paints gaiety on heaven

Birth

she sleeps.
the child inside her
waves to every
passing piece of dream.

and this is morning
where the break of day
insists upon horizons

far ahead of us— this is not a dream.
no candy laden apples
circus gems,
but this is
vast in scope.

New Clothes

I bid goodbye to all
the windswept pins that stood
your hollow rope
falling leaves
your rain
and walked away
as flannel ghosts of new October
danced with empty legs of blue

Pancaked

I sit in a booth
at the Salem Oak diner
the seats are off pink vinyl
a tired hooker's lipstick
waitresses with neck tattoos
carry steaming plates
of other people's satisfaction
I'll never be a rich man
I think to tell the girl
but I can eat and pay rent
in the same week
so let's kill this pig together
I back out in silence
breaking news on the television--
Neil Young has filed for divorce
it's 10 am when my pancakes arrive
and I've yet to hit on the waitress.

We Lit the Stars

we lit the stars
with waxen eyes
candles we could never reach
doctors
white coats
lifting joy--
writing cold prescriptions
for the wakefulness of dreams
today
I pull
the pillow close
and weep
for supernova lust.
we lit the stars
with waxen eyes
and burned the candles down

Standing

the fear is supposed to go away,
at least that's what they tell me.
but there are factors far beyond
the reach
of change.
I am calculating factors
I am translating
as we tremble with anxiety
we are inside heads of infinite scarecrows
and there I stood without a smile
clutching a manuscript of shouts
how did I know about this?
broken telephone
and a dead man's pants—
boots of shit
open paintings on the wall
I want closing but
the fear is supposed to go away.

Wrong Clothes

when everything was of trade
and convenience
when
there was life less cadaverous
and walking
when there was nothing left to kill

— but we slaughtered every one of them

we laid beds out on the table
and slept
we fucked in courses
and we and sang
a thousand songs for royalty

while dressed for knightly comforts
in the dregs of anywhere
all chivalry abandoned us.

For a Moment Eclipsed

she traced compassion on the wrists
like razor wings
Dakini's breath
the narrow space where moments
hold their cold proceedings still--

as Bodhisattvas wept a tear of generation
I watched the transformation

where remembrance left the stage
in the quietude of muffled cold

the heart discarded armor
for she who was the momentary
night illumined
unknown space where all
I thought could never be

was drawn from strokes of feathered eyes
and birthed beneath the rain unseen

Haiku 257

light when morning breaks.
crows fly into the dawn light--
death sings rhapsody

Spring

as Winter dies a little death
and everything of frozen
form is laid again to thaw

here again is something new
it grows a springtime tear
that drops
and wakes
the corpse of hibernation

breath is drawn outside,
and nothing terminal can enter—
Winter dies a little death each and every time.

Astro Phlebotomy

we've bled the present from forever's
determined aptitude
and fed like whorish vampires
without punishments of chains
around us
messiahs handcuffed to their posts—
bedsprings of eternity
temporary flesh,
seeds of momentary reason
planted with an absent mind
a harvest cold and vile

Lying Still

the flies of time have laid their eggs
inside our love
they passed away
beneath the air of change

all that moves a single tear
gas evacuates the husk
too familiar of a scent to ever want again
the gestures of the heart's lone beatings

there is burning in the nostrils
clocks we've damned to move again
and little things that writhe and seep
and hatch in hollow eyes

Dust on the Run

we are exiled from stars
dust on the run
echoes
now vacuous,
carbon on the lamb
prison made of fields and sky
blue water and of rain.

First She Cried

everything was black like winter
trees fell below the sea
and there was you in a circle
of light and of shimmer
in a cusp of new and dawn breaking

but I could not reach you
ancient ritual mantra ties and rope
of old beliefs now falling
cast an oceanic view--
waves atomic and crashing

I gave you the book and you wept
a shedding salt from vajra eyes blue as a saxophone aria

and all I wanted was to make it stop
all I wanted was to know the why
all I wanted was to feel your pain
caress away the sorrow

Derivative

the annals
of meat
are squeezing
the walls
pushing through
phantasms
bone
and delight
where placards
read
enter and
come as you are
and children blow
pinwheels
like Cuisinart blades

Wheels

pieces of the victory
and every bargain made
wholesale disregard

for any of this shit
anymore

take it from me
heaps and mounds
lacking here and apathetic

a slip from all of it

a piece of my dreams
the peel of my heart
these are not for sale today
I piss on your rain-check absolution

tell me how it came to this

I
don't
want
war
but it lives in me
like 100,000 soldiers
dressed in blue with bayonets
marching into this

putting terms to you and I
with blades and with diplomacy
playthings
once of children grown monstrous
in houses made of perfumed tiles
heels pressed hard into the ground

Coup de Etat

the weight
of change
stains of lust
the rock
left bloody
by the road
history does
not die alone
but must
be laid with traitors low
waging their conspiracy
to overthrow today.

Monday

a mid-life shaped by plague and terror
madness and a softer June
a slow-cooking of the bones
a soup
a beef-less water passed for stew

my eyes have bled
my wings have shorn
themselves upon the airy tides
and left my days blown apart where my
ecstasies,
enlightenment,
and stains have all but faded

bedbugs draining
each, my dreams
nips we take into our nights
a younger life shaped by what
we cast for Tuesday's pay

Three

blood stains
on my pillow case
pills
I can't identify
we call this love
a thousand ways
the pulse
is ripe for apathy
sex and cold
dysphoric blades
wedding bands
springtime deaths
winter
in the eyes
of us
red falls ripe on snow

To the Joyful

suffering is not the moment
of the pain
nor anything
of temporal discomforts
that will shit
on us while moving through the day.
suffering is far less sexy than
the razor's edge
the night's last hit
the walk away prompted
by the lack of that last
dollar. suffering
is this here
where moments last forever
and pain is just distraction
tired andfamiliar.

I Was a Small Press Editor

my regards
and apologies
for bringing you
this far
into
a waste
of time
drunk
motherfuckers
and the divorcees
of reason
all pounding keys
because we can

Stage Left

Moses
the abortionist
parted all
you'd ever see
silly girl
you stirred
the pot
with broken thumbs
bones of
splintered solitude
and all
for profit
making change
your births
and your
performance art
we passed
the biohazard hat
around the room and listened

Inpatient

a child
in the trees
I overdosed
on hope and joy
insurmountable
change
this is my
rehab
forever autumnal
and seasoned
with a bit of rain

Lapse

we miss
the past
like
one-night-stands
and gifted
gonorrhea
expired
antibiotics
stains
on our
respectable
pants
amnesia wrapped in tears

Five Days In

on Saturdays we watch movies
on Unit A where the medication
tastes like tears
because the weekend staff doesn't know us
our stories
our laundry routines
blue flannel
       spin cycle
              nervous breakdown
      full of suds
this movie is a repeat
of the one I sat through
last time
not seven months ago
when joy was foreign
this movie doesn't remember me
remember us
we sit with eyes cast upwards
hoping to see ourselves in the credits

Unborn

the appendix to a joy,
you burst like firework-teardrop rain
when all you ever had
was loss
and sold what remained
of empty, brown eyed, beardless
sons— you marched
them off to follow war,
returned to you in pieces

Summer Hanging

two decades gone
he tries in vain
to love a woman
never his
a slip knot falls
the end
of rope
cries aloud
to gravity
less than sums
of every whole--
mathematics of the heart
break down
a null solution every way
now every cord
divides itself again.

Short Change

the mind
is picture
pasted to a dollar frame.
I bought this
on the nickle,
on credit
loaned from memory.

Seepage

you were slipping
        and I could not reach you.
then you fell
you fell so hard
the earth
        beneath
                me shook.
there was freedom
        when I left, imprisoned on return—
the crime was merely one of law;

verdicts in your eyes cast downward,
drilling into bedrock.

Requiem

for all the stars I've seen
and all the stars I've since forgotten,
kissed beneath the sky
and parched of all oblivion,
seraphs bled their tears
and fertilized
a joyous field,
giving life not theirs
into these springtime memories of lust,
synaptic
and forever now--
a tapestry lain
along the pathway leading hard.
our dreams,
our memories,
we bleed into the day.

I Wasn't Born To Starve

I wasn't born to starve
in here
where martyrs clamor,
breadcrumb sins
and eyes of cold
surveillance—
ravens' claws of steel and wire,
scarecrows packed with glycerine.
the dinner plates,
the whites of eyes
we cry before we spit and call
the course of cold anxiety.

It's a Chemical Song

it's a chemical song
and you
were dancing
rhythm
of the afternoon
melodic and dead
and you
were inside me
speaking
in molecular cadence
we frowned
and then we woke up
we drowned
and then we parted ways—
the score
and everything thereafter

Into It

I can't tell if the sun is setting
if I'm rising
where the difference lies between

the fallout of beatitude is noxious
and nerves are spires, rising nowhere—

today a jumper
fell to earth,
and died from disappointment.

Hijacked Grin

they populate the cloud
with reason
bursting
full of rain
and empty kisses in the dawn.

reaching into everywhere
replacing where you've been

the data stacks of tired eyes
to nullify when sleep arrives

a push into the arms of it and
algorithms of the dead
all wave goodbye

Guests

the only angels
come round here
all use my dope and never call—

feathers on the coffee table
empty seats around the fire
cell phone numbers
bits of paper

no one here expects a thing
because the liquor watered down,
cocaine cut with laxative
and furniture brought from the lawn

is not the way to host the night
nor toast the revelation
that our guests are merely dead.

Finish Lines

unconditional and misguided
arms crossed
full of all the indignation
and defiance
heaven ever dared for us to carry

brown fingertips,
my blistered thumb
and ash beneath my nails
extinguishing the mirror's shine

the novel ended there
where you passed the butt
of the gun and said
go first and I will swallow

and dreams of our forever spun around inside the barrel

Fifteen Minutes

I spoke into the machine
you were there
and soulless poems fell

bottles on the floor and empty glasses
high on shelves beyond our reach.
razors in the sinew,

shards of opiated reminiscence
the eyes lain flaccid cast an obelisk of stone

cemetery dances
rings of posies
biohazard muzzles
and we sang with lungs of poison

Diagnosis

this is what I live with
rashes on my back again
receding hairline
fallback front
distention in my belly
and shakes when do one sees me
in darkness where I drank myself to sleep
there is nothing out the door
I sit inside, remembering
remember when the air was good
now frightening
as I take a breath
this is what my life's become
an oxidation growth
repeating itself with hooks and tincture
digging into me
this is what I live with now.
the past is mirrors
cold derision
whistles out of tune somehow

Decomp

something of the dust would
smell cadaverous
organic on the day we told ourselves
all debts had been settled.

because something not alive
could ever be so damned
by imperfection

this is how the rot begins to set
and light becomes
gangrenous
retreating from itself again

Leaving

it was orange in between the sky
and line of rooftop silhouettes
I try to capture time again
on angles made of paper
          made of space

the heart was singularity
unfurled by velvet kiss

now we dance across the table
in stares of constellations

it was blue the day we said goodbye
the skyline rectified itself and time passed into space again

Christmas Eve Shave

a new gray hair
amidst
the speed worn
follicles
I stab
another
grab
another
leave another wanting for
another as we do
this is not a poem
about hair loss
and aging
        the cold and dampened bones again
this is how we start to say
it's Christmas Eve
and no one here
stays up
all night anymore

Carried

there is no more inspiration here
we are a nation of masturbatory fantasy coming
to life in the process of dying
there is nothing to want
nothing to have
you were all that remained in the ash and the embers
the smoke in your eyes was like a mirage
and killing each other
the peak of the pyre
the sweat and perspiration
of desires and of need
were all we knew to make our selves
and everything we cared to carry

Borders of Dust

she spoke of houseplants
window shades and cats
children were a something other
people had on Tuesdays

incarcerated fourteen years
surrounded by the joys of shadow
nothing she can touch in morning
afterglows of tricks
entreats

how the personality
of wavering and mockery
and father left to drink a dream
much better than he could have lived
left it all behind

nurse, oh, nurse please lead us to
the med-cart apparitions
and the tablets torn from bubble packs.
they cannot tally loss today

he strides across
the curtained room
with travesties of rhyme
and palpitations in the boot

she drives

away
in silver cars
that ride
the yellow line's division

Borderline Smiles

she never sought affection
from the stone
that bore maternity,
that left impurities like
schizophrenic husband stains
floor forbidding dance again

she never had attention
from the eyes
that tried to weep
that would not bleed
a tear for all she jeopardized
in wrought unspoken loss
and she
was broken by the stone that made her

gifted her a masquerade
and pantomime to play

with little toys
and wind-up dreams

where mother broke the little girl
chiseled from the very first
transparency of mongoloid and light-defected
shit where mother
was to grow a daughter's soul

what secrets did she hide?
second-hand nightstand shame
in holes where daughter missed her soul

deformities, untreatable like husband death,
tumor struck—
and manufactured nature—
thorazine cries
in police cars
in hospitals, curled up tight
wishing
on a fetal star
she smiles

Passing Checks

it's your silly sense
of usefulness
the hours
of the storm
where tapestry
of lesser days
are dormancy
a moment
catching up
with expectation
moving chips across
the table—
retreat within
the bones of us
precipitation
entropy
and floods across
no ark to sail
no vessel fit
to carry
any one of these
much less
an empty pair of shoes

The Sum in the Solution

she cried when they took away
the only daughter's pillow

screamed when her son at last
knew nothing of the world inside him

there was laughter in the halls of bliss
vacant of the tenants that she knew in darkness well

and haldol injection sites
in the eyes of weekly visitors returning

Thumbnail of an Epic

there were so many,
bent for blood
and slaughter with their swords held high
with tears of rage
and cries of war—
their faces and their tongues carried nothing
but a mournful need
to dismember all they knew,
to flay the feckless face of dawn and birth
a red
forever setting
dusk
where victory and spoils of the day could be forever
tasted, flowing over from the cups
and drinking of the ignorance,
they wrote a drunken history
of valiance and of glory
and spread new generations
to believe it for us all

No Saga

this is entropy
where nothing
bounces back
again
the wounded eyes
of children and
scar tissue of becoming
are the
pantomimes of mockery
and laughter fills the halls of birth
this is entropy at last—
progress
of the surest kind

July Parting

the air would start to smell before it happened
before the monsters hiding
clawed a way through bedtime's feather down

because the breath would gag and scratch our throats
leaving nothing but the bellows
aftertaste of poison

arsenic on your fingertips
a fist full of delivery
a face of invoice
marked for death and signed for with an X

the air would end and nothing smelled
vacuous in memory
and foiled by the arrogance
of ever knowing
what was lost
we wander through the hunting fields—
prey to predatory gods

In the Shadow and the Light

take what's left and run from here;
this home is burning, needful and regretted.

in the nothing where we buried traces
memories and lust, you were everything;
now gone as light from shadows cast.

there are feet entrenched in morning's embers, dying
and a long dark visage thrown ahead of fleeting
footsteps knowing better now than ever,
so run from here and don't return

Of Tin and Toil

the nights when waking feels so far
and days when sleep evades the bones

the sum of Purgatory's calendar written
here between the Earth and sky

       there is not one romantic fucking stitch about it

Hell is us
Heaven is false memory
lapsed

and what we do with dawn and dusk
is work of tired watchmen's hands.

Check Mate

your are my favorite disappointment
scabs I have to pick

and while you punched
my face
I smiled
bleeding

the harder you swung into me
the easier
it was to drift into to a place
where
in my indignation and defense
of self
I exhume the remains
of your pets and ancestors
for rituals, obscene, you'll never know

so hit me harder
I have check

Catacomb

the room was full
of bones rolled hard
in starch
and wrapped in cellophane

no place to bury ghosts
where head stones grew
the names of bastards, mothers,
ghouls alike

now
laid together
and forever to each other,
by umbilical and heart-strung guile
cast on cold and embryonic truths

Fuse

grenades inside the valentines,
land mines in the aisle—
explosions and debris of sentimental gestures
and we were merely ignorant
woeful indestructibility
desirous and in pain
fallout from the time that passed—
the cold macabre backdrop to the scene
we played out
burning film like there
would never be tomorrow
would never be a curtain call
would never be the vulnerable ones
destroyed by all that mattered.

Black Gold

the well went dry,
three miles deep

we drilled ourselves
with carbide gnashing—
tearing through

the tundra's cold defiance
in the face of unrelenting frost.

and everything we knew was buried
somewhere in the slew of night.

Casings

there were casualties
of bullets fired
spent
still smoking
and the
hollow pings
against the wood
popcorn seeds
and
useless things;
stray victims of intended slaughter
pierced by every one of us

Where is Joy

I can't recall
at times
the names
of my own
poems
I write them
and forget them
like prostitutes
who never loved me
left me broke
holding now an empty pen
and souvenir panties.
I stole them somewhere anyhow

Mapped and Topographical

what we called love—
this quantum entanglement,
episodic fucking
to pass the states between,
      and disassociation
      of our faces
from the dead and passing time,
and everything alike we knew

marked us like the beasts we branded;
tethered moments
yokes of sweat—

were strokes of cold dissection
and the moaning of the scalpel raised
searching for the heart became the myth of what was foiled.

Swung

I'm sitting
here in clothes
I haven't
changed
because
I can't
because
the blood
stains
on this shirt
are mine
mementos
of plebeian love
and everything that never was

Methylene

here is where the dying starts
three days into fire and wake
this taste as much like old disease
the tongue of sleep in protest

our base is flooding
blue and yellow
cotton blooms behind the eyes
organic gauze
and sacks of valium,
soaked beyond capacity

flotsam living
far beyond the reach
of breaking waves receding
this is midweek methylene and
nothing new about it

Tablets

whatever gets you off
whatever gets you by
the ebbs of chemical tide and undertow

waves of lithium roll to drown
rising benzo breaths of sleep

I
piss
the night
and all resolve
to photograph the
dark away
and count what I've got left

Last Time

a bottle of ativan,
a bottle of gin,
got halfway through writing
the note

woke up with
an E.R
catheter
stomach pumped
heartbeat blipping
what is this life?

discharged
to a psychiatric
cold delirium
Renoir dream
word-search
colored
crayons
little
nubs of pencil sticks

a two week stay that time around
patched up
detoxed
home with want for more

I still have those

word-search dreams
when rain drip
cloud sound
nightmare loss
puts sweat upon my brow

and all we ever
wanted was more
not to die but feel
alive
in protest of a Nobel Truth
misguided though I failed

Saturday Cleaning

we are
the stale
and tainted
stains
of abortions
gone wild
this carpet
is in sorry shape
as we
unclean
and shameful
now
grow smiles
in the soiled night

Of Her Hair

there were spies in the machinery
ghosts of no one doing nothing
eyes that bled beneath the strokes
projecting vision to the blind

and waking from the final scene
she drank the morning's truthless guile
pulled the drapes away from glass
and witnessed rerun destitution

feet that ran through steam and shower
steps that wove a dancing writ—

she washed the pieces
bath of birth
they remained to reassemble

Words Apart

these are what will not discuss
between the piles bent
in pillows where the ass throbs

violent and devourous
for cocks of time
that pound in Morse code.
these are signals
of distress
these are plumes
rising
mounds like smoke
these are tits

the sun fucks the horizon rising
these are dew drops running corners
of a mouth that says nothing
smiling

words
when there was nothing more to say
nothing to investigate

but genitalia crawls through memory
and playground dreams of dirty knees

these are ancient hands of watchmen
walking long patrols

into growth and embryonic joys

New Class

I am the apathy inside your bones
the ache you just can't place
because you still believe in this
you wake and eat
you fuck in dull boring darkness
and pay your bills with tired ink

I am a generation speaking for the self
I am words you can not hear out loud
I occupy your polished glass
so dear to all that mattered
tarnish on the silver spoon
and I dare of you to taste me now

reflections crack around you
when you have nothing left to say
I would love to lend an ear
when I get sober

Sooner Than Should

I gave up dreams of artistry, of craftsmanship and self.
I gave up dreams of European travels and joy.

I gave up dreams of driving cars--
high speed freeway bliss

and freedoms not afforded in the budget of the heart.
I gave up expectation here of any dreams to come again.

and eyes no longer seem to move
in sleep, if ever sleep would come.

Condemnation

fuck it first
before the shot
sulfur trails

and orifice
menstruating
all experience

onto the moistened
tile grout—
nothing more

to speak of
now
the sentence
punctuated loudly

Waking In Spite

when
night
comes
to the
house
it
brings
tertiary
needles
like
spears
in
punctuation
of a
tapestry
pulled
scratching
on the floor—
morning
is a mess of tracks
none
leading back
to first twilight's well

Coda

she whispers a dream
my ears awake
while cave of sleep surrounding.
does darkness fall eventually,
fall aside and light arise
when heart remembers love?

memories of nothing haunt me
memories of lacking.
but this is the dream
this is the call
to shed the calloused shell.
I reach to touch ethereal love
but fail myself in shame

she whispers a dream
my heart in love
the skin is shedding slowly
darkness damned be gone at last
die as once I followed
when heart remembers love

www.ingramcontent.com/pod-product-compliance
Lightning Source LLC
LaVergne TN
LVHW091238080426
835509LV00009B/1329